DID JESUS RISE FROM THE DEAD?

DID JESUS RISE FROM THE DEAD?

Published by RCpress
ratiochristi.org
2150 Elmwood Ave. Ste 2
Lafayette, IN 47904

© William Lane Craig

Written by William Lane Craigt, PhD
Series Editor: Rick Davy James
Designed by Sam Reynolds

Contributing Editors
Benjamin D. Smith, Jr; Travis Pelletier; Chris Van Allsburg, Derry Teng

Project Management
Kathleen Lovelady

RCpress is the publishing ministry of Ratio Christi, Inc
© 2023 Ratio Christi. All rights reserved. No part of this publication may be reproduced, stored in a retrieval system, or transmitted in any form or by any means, including photocopying, recording, or other electronic or mechanical methods, without the prior permission of RCpress.

ISBN: 978-1-959728-36-8

Adapted from chapter 9 of On Guard *by William Lane Craig*
©2010. Used by permission of David C Cook. May not be further reproduced. All rights reserved.

FAITH & REASON are at odds in our culture. For many, faith has come to mean little more than wishful thinking and blind belief. Such a concept is completely foreign to the pages of Scripture and historical Christianity. As Edward Feser notes, "In short, reason tells us that there is a God and that he has revealed such-and-such a truth; faith is then a matter of believing what reason has shown God to have revealed. In that sense faith is not only not at odds with reason but is grounded in reason."

WHAT IS RATIO CHRISTI?

Ratio Christi, Latin for "the reason of Christ," wants to help reverse this trend of anti-intellectual Christianity. We organize apologetics clubs at colleges, universities, and even for high school groups in order to strengthen the faith of Christian students and faculty and challenge the rampant atheism and secularism on most campuses. Our mission is to fill the intellectual gap, to make Christianity something worth thinking about, both personally and in the public square.

RATIO CHRISTI IS HIRING APOLOGISTS.

Ratio Christi isn't just another apologetics organization. We use our theological training to share the Gospel on college and university campuses across the globe. We reach the people that nobody else can – and we need your help.

ratiochristi.org/join | info@ratiochristi.org

NOTE: *Some of the content in this booklet may not necessarily represent the views of every person involved with, or the official position of, Ratio Christi. Ratio Christi's official statement of faith can be seen at ratiochristi.org/about/beliefs*

It is often said that Christianity stands or falls with the resurrection of Jesus. But here more nuance is needed. Christianity certainly stands or falls with the *event* of Jesus' resurrection. If Jesus did not rise, then he was just another failed Messianic pretender. But Christianity does not stand or fall with the *evidence* for Jesus' resurrection. Most events in history leave no or little evidence of their occurrence. You wouldn't expect that an event like Jesus' resurrection, even if it occurred, would have much, if anything, by way of historical evidence in its favor. It is all the more remarkable, then, just how good a historical case can be made for the historicity of this event. This can give confidence that the event actually occurred.

A historical case for Jesus' resurrection consists of two steps: (i) establishing the facts to be explained, and (ii) assessing the best explanation of the facts.

THE EVIDENCE TO BE EXPLAINED

The evidence to be explained can be summed up under three independently established facts: (1) Jesus' empty tomb, (2) Jesus' appearances alive after his death, and (3) the origin of the disciples' belief in his resurrection. If these three facts can be shown to be historically credible, then the next question to be asked is, "What is the best explanation of these facts?" The explanation given by the earliest followers of Jesus was: "God raised Jesus from the dead." I'll call this the Resurrection Hypothesis. This booklet will explore how this hypothesis compares with rival explanations of the facts. If no plausible, natural explanation can account for them as well as the Resurrection Hypothesis, then one would be justified in inferring Jesus' resurrection is the best explanation of the facts.

(1) The Fact of Jesus' Empty Tomb

Five lines of evidence support the fact Jesus' tomb was found empty by a group of his women followers after his crucifixion.

1. THE HISTORICAL RELIABILITY OF THE STORY OF JESUS' BURIAL SUPPORTS THE EMPTY TOMB. Now you might ask, how does the fact of Jesus' burial prove that his tomb was found empty? The answer is this: if the burial story is basically accurate, then the location of Jesus' tomb was known in Jerusalem to both Jew and Christian alike. But in that case, the tomb must have been empty when the disciples began to preach that Jesus was risen.

Why? *First,* the disciples could not have believed in Jesus' resurrection if his corpse still lay in the tomb. It would have been wholly un-Jewish, not to say stupid, to believe a man was raised from the dead when his body was still in the grave. *Second,* even if the disciples had preached Jesus' resurrection despite his occupied tomb, scarcely anybody else would have believed them. One of the most remarkable facts about the early Christian belief in Jesus' resurrection was that it flourished in the very city where Jesus had been publicly crucified. So long as the people of Jerusalem thought Jesus' body was in the tomb few would have been prepared to believe such nonsense as Jesus had been raised from the dead. And *third,* even if they had so believed, the Jewish authorities would have exposed the whole affair simply by pointing to Jesus' tomb or perhaps even exhuming the body as decisive proof Jesus had not been raised.

The suggestion of some sceptics that the Jewish authorities didn't take this business about Jesus' being risen as anything more than a minor nuisance not worth dealing with is highly implausible and contrary to the evidence. They were deeply concerned about squelching the budding Christian movement (think of their hiring Saul of Tarsus to persecute Jewish Christians!). They would certainly have checked the tomb to see if the corpse was gone.

Even if the remains in the tomb were no longer recognizable, the burden of proof would have been upon anyone who said that these were *not* Jesus' remains. But no such dispute over the identification of Jesus' corpse ever seems to have taken place. As we'll see, the dispute between Jewish non-Christians and Jewish Christians lay elsewhere.

Thus, if the story of Jesus' burial is historical, then it's a very short inference to the fact of the empty tomb as well. For that reason, critics who deny the empty tomb feel compelled to argue against the burial as well. Unfortunately for them, Jesus' burial in the tomb is one of the best-established facts about Jesus. Space doesn't permit all the details of the evidence for the burial but here are a couple points:

First, Jesus' burial is reported in extremely early, independent sources. The account of Jesus' burial in a tomb by Joseph of Arimathea is part of Mark's source material for the Passion Story (the story of Jesus' suffering and death – Mark 15:42-16:8). Since Mark is likely the earliest of the four Gospels, this story derives from a very early source which most scholars think is based on eyewitness testimony.

Moreover, Paul in 1 Corinthians 15:3-4 quotes an old Christian tradition that he had received from the earliest disciples. Paul probably received this tradition no later than his visit to Jerusalem (Galatians 1:18), if not earlier in Damascus. It therefore goes back to within the first five years after Jesus' death. The tradition is a summary of the early Christian preaching and may have been used in instruction because its form was suitable for memorization.

For I delivered to you as of first importance what I also received, that Christ died for our sins according to the Scriptures, and that He was buried, and that He was raised on the third day according to the Scriptures...

Notice the second line of this tradition refers to Jesus' burial.

Further independent testimony to Jesus' burial by Joseph is found in the sources behind Matthew and Luke and in the Gospel of John. The differences between Mark's account of the burial and those of Matthew and Luke suggest that they had sources other than Mark alone. Moreover, we have another independent source for the burial in John's Gospel. Finally, we have the early sermons in the book of Acts, which preserve the early preaching of the apostles. These sermons also mention Jesus' interment in a tomb. Thus, we have the remarkable number of at least five independent sources for Jesus' burial, some of which are extraordinarily early.

Second, as a member of the Jewish Sanhedrin that condemned Jesus, Joseph of Arimathea is unlikely to be a Christian invention. The Sanhedrin was a sort of Jewish high court made up of seventy of the leading men of Judaism, which presided in Jerusalem. The early church had an understandable hostility toward the Sanhedrin. In Christian eyes, they had engineered a judicial murder of Jesus. The sermons in Acts, for example, go so far as to say that the Jewish leaders crucified Jesus (Acts 2:23, 36; 4:10)! Thus, Jesus' burial by Joseph is very probable, since it would be almost inexplicable why Christians would make up a story about a Jewish Sanhedrist who cares properly for Jesus. Joseph is the last person they would choose.

For these and other reasons, most New Testament critics agree that Jesus was buried by Joseph of Arimathea in a tomb. According to the late John A. T. Robinson of Cambridge University, the burial of Jesus in the tomb is "one of the earliest and best-attested facts about Jesus."[1] If this conclusion is correct, then, as I've explained, it's very difficult to deny the fact of the empty tomb.

2. THE DISCOVERY OF JESUS' EMPTY TOMB IS INDEPENDENTLY REPORTED IN VERY EARLY SOURCES.

Mark's Passion source probably didn't end with Jesus' burial but with the women's discovery of Jesus' empty tomb. For the burial story and the empty tomb story are really one story, forming a smooth, continuous narrative linked by grammatical and linguistic ties. Furthermore, it seems unlikely the early Christians would have circulated a story of Jesus' Passion ending in his burial. The Passion story is incomplete without victory at the end. Hence, Mark's source probably included and may have ended with the discovery of the empty tomb.

We've seen that in 1 Corinthians 15:3-5 Paul quotes from an extremely early tradition that refers to Christ's burial and resurrection. Although the empty tomb is not explicitly mentioned, a comparison of the four-line formula with the Gospel narratives on the one hand and the sermons in Acts on the other reveals that the third line is, in fact, a summary of the empty tomb story.

---

1 John A. T. Robinson, *The Human Face of God* (Philadelphia: Westminster, 1973), p. 131.

Moreover, two further features of Paul's tradition imply the empty tomb. First, the expression "he was buried," followed by the expression "he was raised" implies the empty tomb. The idea that a man could be buried and then be raised from the dead and yet his body still remain in the grave is a peculiarly modern notion! For first century Jews there would have been no question but that the tomb of Jesus would have been empty. Therefore, when the tradition states Christ "was buried and he was raised," it automatically implies an empty tomb was left behind. Given the early date and origin of this tradition, its drafters could not have believed such a thing were the tomb not empty.

Second, the expression "on the third day" implies the empty tomb. Very briefly summarized, since no one actually saw Jesus rise from the dead, why did the early disciples proclaim that he had been raised "on the third day"? Why not the seventh day? The most likely answer is that it was on the third day that the women discovered the tomb of Jesus empty; and so naturally, the resurrection itself came to be dated on that day.

We have then, extraordinarily early, independent evidence for the fact of Jesus' empty tomb. The discovery of Jesus' empty tomb cannot be written off as a later legendary development.

But there's more! For once again there are good reasons to discern independent sources for the empty tomb in the other Gospels and Acts. Matthew is clearly working with an independent source for he includes the story of the guard at the tomb, which is unique to his Gospel. Moreover, his comment about how the rumor the disciples had stolen Jesus' body "has been spread among Jews till this day" (Matthew 28:15) shows Matthew is responding to prior tradition. Luke also has an independent source for he tells the story, not found in Mark, of two disciples' visiting the tomb to verify it was vacant. The story can't be regarded as Luke's creation since the incident is independently reported in John. Given John's independence of the other three Gospels, we have yet another independent report of the empty tomb. Finally, in the sermons in the book of Acts, we again have indirect references to the empty tomb. For example, Peter draws the sharp contrast, "David died and was buried and his tomb is with us to this day," but "this Jesus God has raised up" (Acts 2:29-32; compare 13:36-7).

Historians think they've hit historical pay-dirt when they have two independent accounts of the same event. But in the case of the empty tomb we have no less than six, and some of these are among the earliest materials to be found in the New Testament.

3. MARK'S STORY IS SIMPLE AND LACKS LEGENDARY DEVELOPMENT. Like the burial account, Mark's account of the empty tomb is remarkably simple and unembellished by theological motifs likely to characterize a later legendary account. For example, the resurrection is not witnessed or described, and there's no reflection on Jesus' triumph over sin and death, no use of divine titles, no quotation of fulfilled prophecy, no description of the Risen Lord. It's very different than a Christian fictional creation—just compare how the resurrection is portrayed in modern Passion plays!

To appreciate how restrained Mark's narrative is you only have to read the account in the apocryphal Gospel of Peter which describes Jesus' triumphant exit from the tomb as a gigantic figure whose head reaches above the clouds, supported by giant angels, followed by a talking cross, heralded by a voice from heaven, and all witnessed by a Roman guard, the Jewish leaders, and a multitude of spectators! This is how real legends look: they're colored by theological and historical exaggerations. By contrast, Mark's account is stark in its simplicity.

4. THE TOMB WAS PROBABLY DISCOVERED EMPTY BY WOMEN. In order to grasp this point, two things need to be understood about the place of women in Jewish society.

First, women were not regarded as credible witnesses. This attitude toward the testimony of women is evident in the Jewish historian Josephus' description of the rules for admissible testimony: "Let not the testimony of women be admitted, on account of the levity and boldness of their sex" (*Antiquities* IV.8.15). No such regulation is to be found in the Bible. It is rather a reflection of the patriarchal society of first century Judaism.

Second, women occupied a low rung on the Jewish social ladder. Compared to men, women were second-class citizens. Consider these rabbinical texts: "Sooner let the words of the Law be burnt than delivered to women!" (Sotah 19a) and again: "Happy is he whose children are male, but unhappy is he whose children are female!" (Kiddushin 82b). The daily prayer of every Jewish man included the blessing, "Blessed are you, Lord our God, ruler of the universe, who has not created me a Gentile, a slave, or a woman" (Berachos 60b).

So, given their low social status and inability to serve as legal witnesses, it's quite amazing that *women* are the discoverers of and principal witnesses to the empty tomb. If the empty tomb story were a legend, then the male disciples would have been made to be the ones who discover the empty tomb. The fact that women, whose testimony was deemed worthless, were the chief witnesses to the fact of the empty tomb can only be plausibly explained if, like it or not, they actually were the discoverers of the empty tomb, and the Gospels faithfully recorded what for them was a very embarrassing fact.

5. THE EARLIEST JEWISH RESPONSE PRESUPPOSES THE EMPTY TOMB. In Matthew 28:11-15 we find an attempt to refute the earliest Jewish response to the Christian proclamation of the resurrection. Now our interest is not so much in the guard at the tomb as in Matthew's incidental remark at the end, "this story was widely spread among the Jews, and is to this day." This remark reveals that the author was concerned to refute a widespread Jewish explanation of the resurrection.

What were unbelieving Jews saying in response to the disciples' proclamation that Jesus was risen? That these men were full of new wine? That Jesus' body still lay in the tomb in the garden? No. They were saying, "His disciples came by night and stole Him away." The Jewish authorities did not deny the empty tomb but instead entangled themselves in a hopeless series of absurdities trying to explain it away. In other words, the Jewish claim the disciples had stolen the body presupposes the body was missing. This is evidence for the fact of the empty tomb which is really top-drawer because it comes, not from the followers of Jesus, but from the very opponents of the early Jesus movement.

Taken together these five lines of evidence constitute a powerful case Jesus' tomb was, indeed, found empty on the first day of the week by a group of his women followers. As a historical fact, this seems to be well-established. According to Jacob Kremer, a New Testament critic who has specialized in the study of the resurrection, "By far most scholars hold firmly to the reliability of the biblical statements about the empty tomb."[2] In fact, in a survey of over 2,200 publications on the resurrection in English, French, and German since 1975, Gary Habermas found that 75% of scholars accepted the historicity of the discovery of Jesus' empty tomb.[3] The evidence is so compelling that even a number of Jewish scholars, such as Pinchas Lapide and Geza Vermes, have declared themselves convinced on the basis of the evidence that Jesus' tomb was found empty.

(2) The Fact of Jesus' Post-Mortem Appearances

In 1 Corinthians 15:3-8, Paul writes:

For I delivered to you as of first importance what I also received, that Christ died for our sins according to the Scriptures, and that He was buried, and that He was raised on the third day according to the Scriptures, and that He appeared to Cephas, then to the twelve. After that He appeared to more than five hundred brethren at one time, most of whom remain until now, but some have fallen asleep; then He appeared to James, then to all the apostles; and last of all, as to one untimely born, He appeared to me also.

This is a truly remarkable claim. We have here an indisputably authentic letter of a man personally acquainted with the first disciples, and he reports they actually saw Jesus alive after his death. More than that, he says he himself also saw an appearance of Jesus. What are we to make of this claim? Did Jesus really appear to people alive after his death?

To answer this question, consider three main lines of evidence for the resurrection appearances of Jesus.

---

2 Jacob Kremer, *Die Osterevangelien—Geschichten um Geschichte* (Stuttgart: Katholisches Bibelwerk, 1977), pp. 49-50.
3 Gary Habermas, "Experience of the Risen Jesus: The Foundational Historical Issue in the Early Proclamation of the Resurrection," *Dialog* 45 (2006): 292.

1. **PAUL'S LIST OF EYEWITNESSES TO JESUS' RESURRECTION APPEARANCES SHOWS THAT SUCH APPEARANCES OCCURRED.** In 1 Corinthians 15 Paul gives a list of witnesses to Jesus' resurrection appearances. Is it plausible such events actually took place?

Appearance to Peter: We have no story in the Gospels telling of Jesus' appearance to Peter, but the appearance is mentioned here in the old Christian tradition quoted by Paul, which originated in the Jerusalem church, and it's vouched for by the apostle Paul himself. As we know from Galatians 1:18, Paul spent about two weeks with Peter in Jerusalem three years after his conversion on the Damascus Road. So Paul knew personally whether Peter claimed to have had such an experience or not. In addition to this, the appearance to Peter is mentioned in another old Christian tradition found in Luke 24:34: "The Lord has really risen, and has appeared to Simon!" That Luke is passing on a prior tradition here is evident from the awkward way in which it is inserted into his story of the appearance to the Emmaus disciples. So although we have no story of the appearance to Peter, it is quite well-founded historically. As a result, virtually all New Testament critics agree Peter saw an appearance of Jesus alive from the dead.

Appearance to the Twelve: Undoubtedly, the group referred to here is the original group of twelve disciples who had been chosen by Jesus during his ministry—minus, of course, Judas, whose absence didn't affect the formal title of the group. This is the best attested resurrection appearance of Jesus. It, too, is included in the very early traditional formula that Paul cites, and Paul himself had contact with members of the Twelve. Moreover, we have independent stories of this appearance in Luke 24:36-42 and John 20:19-20. Undoubtedly, the most notable feature of these appearance stories is the physical demonstrations of Jesus showing his wounds and eating before the disciples. The purpose of the physical demonstrations is to show two things: first, Jesus was raised *physically*; and second, he was the *same Jesus* who had been crucified. There can be little doubt such an appearance occurred, for it is attested in the old Christian tradition, vouched for by Paul, who had personal contact with the Twelve, and is independently described by both Luke and John.

Appearance to 500 brethren: The third appearance comes as something of a shock: "He appeared to more than five hundred brethren at one time"! This is surprising, since we have no mention whatsoever of this appearance elsewhere in the New Testament. This might make us rather skeptical about this appearance, but Paul apparently had personal contact with these people since he knew some had died. Why does Paul add that some are still alive? The great New Testament scholar of Cambridge University, C. H. Dodd, replies, "There can hardly be any purpose in mentioning the fact that the most of the 500 are still alive, unless Paul is saying, in effect, 'The witnesses are there to be questioned.'"[4] Notice: Paul could never have said this if the event had not occurred.

---

4 C. H. Dodd, "The Appearances of the Risen Christ: A study in the form criticism of the Gospels," in *More New Testament Studies* (Manchester: University of Manchester, 1968), p. 128.

He would not have challenged people to talk to the witnesses if the event had never taken place and there were no witnesses. Therefore, the event must have taken place.

I suspect this appearance is not related in the Gospels because it probably took place in Galilee. As one puts together the various appearances in the Gospels, it seems they occurred first in Jerusalem, then in Galilee, and then in Jerusalem again. In Galilee thousands had gathered to hear Jesus teach during his ministry. Since the Gospels focus their attention on the appearances in Jerusalem, we don't have any story of this appearance to the 500. An intriguing possibility is that this was the appearance predicted by the angel at the tomb and described by Matthew (28.16-17).

Appearance to James: The next appearance is one of the most amazing of all. Jesus appeared to James, his younger brother. What makes this amazing is that apparently neither James nor any of Jesus' younger brothers believed in Jesus during his lifetime (Mark 3:21, 31-35; John 7:1-10). They didn't believe he was the Messiah, or a prophet, or even anybody special. By the criterion of embarrassment, this is doubtless a historical fact of Jesus' life and ministry.

After the resurrection, Jesus' brothers show up in the Christian fellowship in the upper room in Jerusalem (Acts 1:14). There's no further mention of them until Acts 12:17, the story of Peter's deliverance from prison by the angel. What are Peter's first words? "Report this to *James*." In Galatians 1:19 Paul tells of his two-week visit to Jerusalem about three years after his Damascus Road experience. He says that besides Peter he saw none of the other apostles *except James* the Lord's brother. When Paul visited Jerusalem again fourteen years later he says there were three "pillars" of the church in Jerusalem: Peter, John, and *James* (Galatians 2:9). Finally, in Acts 21:18 James is the sole head of the Jerusalem church and the council of elders. We hear no more about James in the New Testament; but from Josephus, the Jewish historian, we learn James was stoned to death illegally by the Sanhedrin after AD 60 for his faith in Christ (*Antiquities* 20.200).

Jesus' other brothers also became believers and were active in Christian preaching, as we see from 1 Corinthians 9:5: "Do we not have a right to take along a believing wife, even as the rest of the apostles and the brothers of the Lord and Cephas?"

Now, how is this to be explained? On the one hand, it seems certain that Jesus' brothers did not believe in him during his lifetime. On the other hand, it's equally certain that they became ardent Christians, active in ministry. Jesus' crucifixion would only confirm in James' mind that his elder brother's Messianic pretensions were delusory, just as he had thought. Many of us have brothers. What would it take to make you believe your brother is the Lord, so that you would die for this belief, as James did? Can there be any doubt the reason for this remarkable transformation is to be found in the fact "then he appeared to James"? Even the sceptical New Testament critic Hans Grass admits the conversion of James is one of the surest proofs of the resurrection of Jesus.[5]

Appearance to "all the apostles": This appearance was probably to a limited circle of

---

5 Hans Grass, *Ostergeschehen und Osterberichte*, 4th ed. (Göttingen: Vandenhoeck & Ruprecht, 1974), p. 80.

Christian missionaries somewhat wider than the Twelve. For such a group, see Acts 1:21-22. Once again, the fact of this appearance is guaranteed by Paul's personal contact with the apostles themselves.

Appearance to Saul of Tarsus: The final appearance is just as amazing as the appearance to James: "And last of all," says Paul, "He appeared to me also." The story of Jesus' appearance to Saul of Tarsus (or Paul) just outside Damascus is related in Acts 9:1-9 and is later told again twice. That this event occurred is established beyond doubt by Paul's references to it in his own letters.

This event changed Saul's whole life. He was a rabbi, a Pharisee, a respected Jewish leader. He hated the Christian heresy and did everything in his power to stamp it out. He tells us he was even responsible for the *execution* of Christian believers. Then suddenly he gave up everything. He left his position as a respected Jewish leader and became a Christian missionary: he entered a life of poverty, labor, and suffering. He was whipped, beaten, stoned and left for dead, shipwrecked three times, in constant danger, deprivation, and anxiety. Finally, he made the ultimate sacrifice and was martyred for his faith at Rome. And it was all because on that day outside Damascus he saw "Jesus our Lord" (1 Cor. 9:1).

In summary, Paul's testimony makes it historically certain that various individuals and groups of people experienced appearances of Jesus after his death and burial.

2. THE GOSPEL ACCOUNTS PROVIDE MULTIPLE, INDEPENDENT REPORTS OF POST-MORTEM APPEARANCES OF JESUS. The Gospels independently report post-mortem appearances of Jesus, even some of the same appearances found in Paul's list. The appearance to Peter is independently mentioned by Paul and Luke (1 Corinthians 15.5; Luke 24.34) and is universally acknowledged by critics. The appearance to the Twelve is independently reported by Paul, Luke, and John (1 Corinthians 15.5; Luke 24:36-43; John 20.19-20) and is again not in dispute. The appearance to the women disciples is independently reported by Matthew and John (Matthew 28.9-10; John 20.11-17) and enjoys ratification by the criterion of embarrassment, given the low credibility accorded to the testimony of women. It's generally agreed the absence of this appearance from the list of appearances in the tradition quoted by Paul is a reflection of the discomfort in citing female witnesses. Finally, that Jesus appeared to the disciples in Galilee is independently reported by Mark, Matthew, and John (Mark 16.7; Matthew 28:16-17; John 21).

Taken sequentially, the appearances follow the pattern of Jerusalem—Galilee—Jerusalem, matching the pilgrimages of the disciples as they returned to Galilee following the Passover/Feast of Unleavened Bread and then traveled again to Jerusalem two months later for Pentecost.

From this evidence what should we conclude? We can call the appearances hallucinations, but we cannot deny they occurred. Even the sceptical critic Gerd Lüdemann is emphatic: "It may be taken as historically certain that Peter and the disciples had experiences after Jesus' death in which Jesus appeared to them as the risen Christ."[6] The evidence makes it certain that on separate occasions different individuals and groups experienced seeing Jesus alive from the dead. This conclusion is virtually indisputable.

3. THE RESURRECTION APPEARANCES WERE PHYSICAL, BODILY APPEARANCES.

So far the evidence we've examined doesn't depend on the nature of the post-mortem appearances of Jesus. I've left it open whether they were visionary or physical in nature. It remains to be seen whether visionary experiences of the risen Jesus can be plausibly explained on purely psychological grounds. But if the appearances were physical and bodily in nature, then a purely psychological explanation becomes next to impossible. So it is worth examining what we can know about the nature of these appearances.

Paul implies that the appearances were physical. He does this in two ways.

First, he conceives of the resurrection body as physical. Everyone recognizes that Paul does not teach the immortality of the soul alone but the resurrection of the *body*. In 1 Corinthians 15:42-44 Paul describes the differences between the present, earthly body and our future, resurrection body, which will be like Christ's. He draws four essential contrasts between the earthly body and the resurrection body:

EARTHLY BODY IS:	RESURRECTION BODY IS:
mortal	immortal
dishonorable	glorious
weak	powerful
natural	spiritual

Only the last contrast could possibly make us think that Paul did not believe in a physical resurrection body. But what does he mean by the words translated here as "natural/spiritual"?

The word translated "natural" literally means "soul-ish." Now obviously, Paul doesn't mean that our present body is made out of soul. Rather, by this word he means "dominated by or pertaining to human nature." Similarly, when he says the resurrection body will be "spiritual," he doesn't mean "made out of spirit." Rather, he means "dominated by or oriented toward the Spirit." It's the same sense of the word "spiritual" as when we say that someone is a spiritual person.

---

6 Gerd Lüdemann, *What Really Happened to Jesus?*, trans. John Bowden (Louisville, Kent.: Westminster John Knox Press, 1995), p. 80.

Look at how Paul uses the same words in 1 Corinthians 2:14-15:

But a natural man does not accept the things of the Spirit of God, for they are foolishness to him; and he cannot understand them, because they are spiritually appraised. But he who is spiritual appraises all things, yet he himself is appraised by no one.

Natural man does not mean "physical, visible man," but "man oriented toward human nature." And *spiritual man* does not mean "intangible, invisible man" but "man oriented toward the Spirit." The contrast is the same in 1 Corinthians 15. The present, earthly body will be freed from its slavery to the mortal nature and become instead fully empowered and directed by God's Spirit. Thus, Paul's doctrine of the resurrection body implies a physical resurrection.

Second, Paul, and indeed all the New Testament, makes a distinction between an *appearance* of Jesus and a vision of Jesus. The appearances of Jesus soon ceased, but visions of Jesus continued in the early church. Now the question is: what is the difference between an appearance and a vision? The NT seems to be clear: a vision, though caused by God, was purely in the mind, while an appearance took place "out there" in the external world.

Compare Stephen's vision of Jesus in Acts 7 with the resurrection appearances of Jesus. Though Stephen saw an identifiable, bodily image, what he saw was a vision of a man, not a man who was physically there, for no one else present experienced anything at all. By contrast the resurrection appearances took place in the world "out there" and could be experienced by anybody present. Paul could rightly regard his experience on the Damascus Road as an appearance, even though it took place after Jesus' ascension, because it involved manifestations in the external world like the light and the voice, which Paul's companions also experienced to varying degrees. Thus, the distinction between a vision and an appearance of Jesus also implies that the resurrection appearances were physical.

The Gospel accounts show that the appearances were physical and bodily. Again, two points deserve to be made.

First, every resurrection appearance related in the Gospels is a physical bodily appearance. The unanimous testimony of the Gospel in this regard is quite impressive. If none of the appearances were originally a physical bodily appearance, then it's very strange we have a completely unanimous testimony in the Gospels that all of them were physical with no trace of the supposed original non-physical appearances.

Second, if all the appearances were originally non-physical visions, then we're at a complete loss to explain the rise of the Gospel accounts. For physical, bodily appearances would be foolishness to Gentiles and a stumbling block to Jews, since neither could accept physical resurrection from the dead, but both would have been quite happy to accept visionary appearances of the deceased.

To be perfectly candid, the only grounds for denying the physical, bodily nature of the post-mortem appearances of Jesus are philosophical, not historical. Such appearances would be miracles of the most stupendous proportions that many critics cannot swallow. But in that case we need to re-trace our steps to think again about the evidence for the existence of God. If God exists, there's no good reason to be skeptical about miracles. In our debate, agnostic Australian philosopher Peter Slezak nicely put it, for a God who is able to create the entire universe, the odd resurrection would be child's play! Most New Testament critics are unfortunately untrained in philosophy and are, hence, naive when it comes to these issues.

So, on the basis of these lines of evidence, we can conclude that the fact of Jesus' post-mortem appearances to various individuals and groups under a variety of circumstances is firmly established historically and, moreover, that these appearances were bodily and physical.

(3) The Fact of the Origin of the Christian Faith

The third fact to be explained is the very origin of the Christian faith. We all know Christianity sprang into being sometime midway through the first century after Christ. Why did it come into existence? What caused this movement to begin? Even skeptical New Testament scholars recognize the Christian faith owes its origin to the belief of the earliest disciples, that God had raised Jesus of Nazareth from the dead. In fact, they pinned nearly everything on this belief.

To take just one example: Jews had no conception of a Messiah who, instead of triumphing over Israel's enemies, would be shamefully executed by them as a criminal. Messiah was supposed to be a triumphant figure who would command the respect of Jew and Gentile alike and who would establish the throne of David in Jerusalem. To them, a Messiah who failed to deliver and to reign, who was defeated, humiliated, and slain by his enemies, is a contradiction in terms. Therefore, it's difficult to overemphasize what a disaster the crucifixion was for the disciples' faith. Jesus' death on the cross spelled the humiliating end for any hopes they had entertained he was the Messiah.

But the belief in the resurrection of Jesus reversed the catastrophe of the crucifixion. Because God had raised Jesus from the dead, he was seen to be Messiah after all. Thus, Peter proclaims in Acts 2:23-24, 36, "this *Man*... you nailed to a cross by the hands of godless men and put *Him* to death. But God raised Him up again... Therefore let all the house of Israel know for certain that God has made Him both Lord and Christ." It was on the basis of belief in his resurrection that the disciples could believe Jesus was the Messiah.

It's no surprise therefore, that belief in Jesus' resurrection was universal in the early Christian church. The traditional formula quoted in 1 Corinthians 15:3-7, in which the

Gospel is defined as the death, burial, resurrection, and appearances of Christ, shows this understanding of the Gospel goes right back to the very beginning of the church in Jerusalem.

Thus, the origin of Christianity hinges on the belief of the earliest disciples that God had raised Jesus from the dead. But the question is: How does one explain the origin of that belief? As R. H. Fuller says, even the most skeptical critic must posit some mysterious X to get the movement going.[7] But what was that X?

Now we're ready to summarize all three of our points:

First, we saw that numerous lines of historical evidence indicate that the tomb of Jesus was found empty by a group of his women followers.

Second, we saw that several lines of historical evidence establish that on numerous occasions and in different places various individuals and groups saw appearances of Jesus alive from the dead.

And finally, third, we saw that the very origin of the Christian faith depends on the belief of the earliest disciples that God had raised Jesus of Nazareth from the dead.

One of the things that most astonished me after completing my doctoral research at the University of Munich on Jesus' resurrection was the realization these three great, independently established facts represent *the majority view* of New Testament critics today. The only point of serious disagreement would be on the physical nature of the resurrection appearances. But the state of current scholarship strongly supports the three facts as I have stated them.

These are not the conclusions of conservative or evangelical scholarship; these are the conclusions of mainstream New Testament criticism. As we saw, three-quarters of scholars who have written on the subject accept the fact of the empty tomb; virtually no one today denies that the earliest disciples experienced post-mortem appearances of Jesus; and far and away most scholars agree the earliest disciples at least believed God had raised Jesus from the dead. It is the critic who would deny these facts that today finds himself on the defensive.

It's worth noticing that the historicity of these three facts is not affected by inconsistencies in the circumstantial details of the Gospel accounts. The three facts are well-established even given conflicts in the secondary details. Historians expect to find inconsistencies even in the most reliable sources. No historian simply throws out a source because it has inconsistencies. Otherwise we'd have to be skeptical about all secular historical narratives which also contain such inconsistencies, which is wholly unreasonable. Moreover, in the case of the four Gospels the inconsistencies aren't even within a single source; they're between independent sources. But obviously, it doesn't follow from an inconsistency between two independent sources that both sources are wrong. At worst, one is wrong if they can't be harmonized. Minor discrepancies in the narratives thus don't affect the historicity of the three facts as I have stated them.

---

7 R. H. Fuller, *The Formation of the Resurrection Narratives* (London: SPCK, 1972), p. 2.

Actually, the Gospels narratives are largely consistent. All four Gospels attest to these facts: Jesus of Nazareth was crucified in Jerusalem by Roman authority during the Passover Feast, having been arrested and convicted on charges of blasphemy by the Jewish Sanhedrin and then slandered before the governor Pilate on charges of treason. He died within several hours and was buried Friday afternoon by Joseph of Arimathea in a tomb, which was shut with a stone. Certain women followers of Jesus, including Mary Magdalene, having observed his interment, visited his tomb early on Sunday morning, only to find it empty. Thereafter, Jesus appeared alive from the dead to the disciples, including Peter, who then became proclaimers of the message of his resurrection.

The remaining question then, is how the three established facts I've stated are best explained.

EXPLAINING THE EVIDENCE

We come, then, to the second step: determining which explanation of the evidence is the best. Historians weigh various factors in assessing competing hypotheses. Some of the most important are as follows:[8]

1. The best explanation will have the greatest *explanatory scope*. That is, it will explain more evidence than other explanations.
2. The best explanation will have the greatest *explanatory power*. That is, it will make the evidence more probable.
3. The best explanation will be the most *plausible explanation*. That is, it will fit better with true background beliefs.
4. The best explanation will be the least *contrived*. That is, it won't require adopting as many new beliefs which have no independent evidence.
5. The best explanation will be *disconfirmed by fewer accepted beliefs* than other explanations. That is, it won't conflict with as many accepted beliefs.
6. The best explanation will meet conditions (1) – (5) so much better than the others that there's little chance one of the other explanations, after further investigation, will do better.

Since a hypothesis may do really well meeting some conditions but not so well meeting others, figuring out which hypothesis is the best explanation may be difficult. But if the explanatory scope and power of a hypothesis are very great, so that it explains a wide variety of facts, then it's likely to be true.

So let's apply these tests to the typical hypotheses which have been offered down through history to explain the empty tomb, post-mortem appearances, and origin of the disciples' belief in Jesus' resurrection, and see if they do better, or as well, in explaining these facts as the Resurrection Hypothesis.

Conspiracy Hypothesis

According to this hypothesis, the disciples stole the body of Jesus and lied about his appearances, thus faking the resurrection. This was the very first counter-explanation

---

8 C. Behan McCullagh, *Justifying Historical Descriptions* (Cambridge: Cambridge University Press, 1984), p. 19.

for the empty tomb and it was revived during the eighteenth century by European Deists. Today, however, this explanation has been completely given up by modern scholarship.

1. EXPLANATORY SCOPE. The Conspiracy Hypothesis does seem to cover the full scope of the evidence, for it offers explanations of the empty tomb (the disciples stole the body), the post-mortem appearances (the disciples lied), and the origin of the disciples' (supposed) belief in Jesus' resurrection (again, they lied).

2. EXPLANATORY POWER. How probable is the evidence, given the Conspiracy Hypothesis? Here doubts begin to arise about the adequacy of the hypothesis.

First, consider the story of the empty tomb. If the disciples stole Jesus' corpse, then it would be utterly pointless to fabricate a story about *women* finding the tomb to be empty. Such a story would not be the sort of tale Jewish men would invent. Moreover, the simplicity of the story is not what one would expect. Where are the Scriptural proof-texts? Why isn't Jesus described as emerging from the tomb, as in later forgeries like the Gospel of Peter? A fabricator would probably describe Jesus' resurrection appearances in terms of Old Testament visions of God and descriptions of the end-time resurrection (as in Daniel 12:2). But then Jesus should appear to the disciples in dazzling glory. And why not a description of the resurrection itself?

But the explanatory power of the Conspiracy Hypothesis is undoubtedly weakest when it comes to the origin of the disciples' belief in Jesus' resurrection. For the hypothesis is really a denial of that fact. But as critics have universally recognized, you can't plausibly deny that the earliest disciples at least sincerely *believed* Jesus was risen from the dead. They staked their very lives on that conviction. The transformation in the lives of the disciples is not credibly explained by the hypothesis of a conspiracy. This shortcoming alone has been enough in the minds of most scholars to sink the old Conspiracy Hypothesis forever.

3. PLAUSIBILITY. The real Achilles' heel of the Conspiracy Hypothesis is its implausibility. The unbelievable complexity of such a conspiracy or the supposed psychological state of the disciples is difficult enough to believe, but the overriding problem that dwarfs all others is that it is wholly anachronistic to suppose first century Jews intended to hoax Jesus' resurrection. The Conspiracy Hypothesis views the disciples' situation through the rearview mirror of Christian history rather than through the eyes of a Jew.

In the first place, there was no expectation in Judaism of a Messiah who, instead of establishing David's throne and subduing Israel's enemies, would be shamefully executed by the Gentiles as a criminal. The Jewish idea of resurrection was just unconnected from the idea of Messiah and even incompatible with it, since Messiah was not supposed to be killed.

Secondly, the Jewish conception of resurrection differed in at least two fundamental respects from the resurrection of Jesus.

First, in Jewish thinking the resurrection to glory and immortality always occurred *after* the end of the world. Jews had no idea of a resurrection within history. That's why the disciples had so much trouble understanding Jesus' predictions of his own resurrection. They thought he was talking about the resurrection at the end of the world. Look at Mark 9:9-11, for example.

> *As they were coming down from the mountain, He gave them orders not to relate to anyone what they had seen, until the Son of Man rose from the dead. They seized upon that statement, discussing with one another what rising from the dead meant. They asked Him, saying,* "Why is it *that the scribes say that Elijah must come first?"*

Here Jesus predicts his resurrection, and what do the disciples ask? "*Why is it* that the scribes say that Elijah must come first?" In first century Judaism it was believed the prophet Elijah would come again before the great and terrible Day of the Lord, the judgment day when the dead would be raised. The disciples could not understand the idea of a resurrection prior to the end of the world. Hence, Jesus' predictions only confused them. Thus, given the Jewish conception of the resurrection, the disciples after Jesus' crucifixion would not have come up with a bodily resurrection.

Second, in Jewish thinking the resurrection was always the resurrection of all the righteous dead. Jews had no idea of the resurrection of an isolated individual apart from the general resurrection. Moreover, there was simply no connection between the individual believer's resurrection and the prior resurrection of the Messiah. That's why we find no examples of other failed messianic movements claiming that their executed leader was risen from the dead. Wright has been insistent upon this point:

> *All the followers of those first century messianic movements were fanatically committed to the cause… But in no case right across the century before Jesus and the century after him do we hear of any Jewish group saying that their executed leader had been raised from the dead…*[9]

So the idea of stealing Jesus' corpse and saying God had raised him from the dead is hardly one that would have entered the minds of these Jewish disciples of Jesus nor seemed to them a plausible strategy for evangelizing their fellow Jews!

But, what about influences from outside Judaism? A suggestion widespread on the internet today is that early Christians came up with the idea of Jesus' resurrection through the influence of pagan mythology. This suggestion is an old one. Back around the turn of the 19th to the 20th century, scholars in comparative religion collected parallels to Christian beliefs in other religious movements, and some even thought to explain

---

9 N. T. Wright, lecture at Asbury College and Seminary, 1999.

Christian beliefs, including the belief in Jesus' resurrection, as the result of the influence of such myths. The movement soon collapsed, however, principally due to two factors:

First, scholars came to realize that the parallels are false. The ancient world was a virtual fruit basket of myths of various gods and heroes. Comparative studies in religion require sensitivity to their similarities *and differences*, or distortion and confusion inevitably result. Unfortunately, those who were eager to find parallels to Jesus' resurrection failed to exercise such sensitivity.

Many of the alleged parallels are actually stories of the *assumption* of the hero into heaven (Hercules, Romulus). Others are *disappearance* stories, which claim the hero has vanished into a higher sphere (Apollonius of Tyana, Empedocles). Still others are *seasonal symbols* for the crop cycle, as the vegetation dies in the dry season and comes back to life in the rainy season (Tammuz, Osiris, Adonis). Some are *political expressions* of Emperor worship (Julius Caesar, Caesar Augustus).

None of these ideas is parallel to the Jewish idea of the resurrection of the dead. Most scholars have come to doubt whether there really were *any* myths of dying and rising gods at all. For example, in the myth of Osiris, which was one of the best known symbolic seasonal myths, Osiris doesn't really come back to life but simply continues to exist in the realm of the dead.

Pagan mythology is simply the wrong interpretive context for understanding Jesus of Nazareth. Jesus and his disciples were first century Jews, and they must be understood against that background.

Second, there is in any case no causal connection between the pagan myths and the origin of the disciples' belief in Jesus' resurrection. Jews were familiar with the seasonal pagan deities (Ezekiel 8.14-15) and found them abhorrent. That's why there is no trace of cults with dying and rising gods at all in first century Israel. It's pretty unlikely the original disciples would have come up with the idea that Jesus was risen from the dead because they had heard pagan myths about dying and rising seasonal deities. So scholars have universally abandoned this approach. Internet sceptics are over 100 years out of date.

Notice that this criticism undermines not only conspiracy theories, which suppose the disciples *insincerely* proclaimed Jesus' resurrection, but also any theory which suggests that, on the basis of pagan or Jewish influences, they *sincerely* came to believe in and preached his resurrection.

4. LESS CONTRIVED. The Conspiracy Hypothesis supposes that all the evidence seems to point to mere appearance only, explained away by hypotheses for which there is no evidence. Specifically, it postulates motives and ideas in the minds of the earliest disciples and actions on their part for which there is not a shred of evidence. It can become even more contrived, as hypotheses have to be multiplied to deal with objections to the theory, for example, how to account for the appearance to the 500 brethren or the women's role in the empty tomb and appearance stories.

5. Disconfirmed by fewer accepted beliefs. The Conspiracy Hypothesis tends to be disconfirmed by our general knowledge of conspiracies, their instability and tendency to unravel. Moreover, it is disconfirmed by the sincerity of the disciples and the nature of first century Jewish messianic expectations.

6. Exceeds other hypotheses in fulfilling conditions (1) – (5). This condition is obviously not met, since there are better hypotheses (such as the Hallucination Hypothesis), which don't dismiss the disciples' belief in Jesus' resurrection as a blatant lie.

No scholar would defend the Conspiracy Hypothesis today. The only place you read about such things is in the popular, sensationalist press or on the internet.

Apparent Death Hypothesis

A second suggested explanation was the Apparent Death Hypothesis. Critics around the beginning of the nineteenth century claimed Jesus was not completely dead when he was taken down from the cross. He revived in the tomb and escaped to convince his disciples he had risen from the dead.

This hypothesis has also been almost completely given up.

1. Explanatory scope. The Apparent Death Hypothesis provides explanations for the empty tomb, post-mortem appearances, and the disciples' belief in Jesus' resurrection.

2. Explanatory power. Here the theory begins to founder. Some versions of the Apparent Death Hypothesis were really variations on the Conspiracy Hypothesis. Instead of stealing the body, the disciples (along with Jesus himself!) were supposed to have conspired to fake Jesus' death on the cross. In that case the theory shares all the weaknesses of the Conspiracy Hypothesis.

A non-conspiratorial version of the theory was that Jesus just happened to survive the crucifixion, though the guards thought he was dead. Such a version of the hypothesis is saddled with insurmountable difficulties: How do you explain the empty tomb, since a man sealed inside a tomb could not move the stone to escape? How do you explain the post-mortem appearances, since the appearance of a half-dead man desperately in need of medical attention would hardly have elicited the conclusion he was the Risen Lord and conqueror of Death? How do you explain the origin of the disciples' belief in Jesus' resurrection, since seeing him again would only lead them to conclude he had not died, not that he was, contrary to Jewish thought, gloriously risen from the dead?

3. **Plausibility.** Here again the theory fails miserably. Roman executioners could be relied upon to ensure their victims were dead. Since the exact moment of death by crucifixion is uncertain, executioners could ensure death by a spear thrust into the victim's side as they did to Jesus (John 19.34). Moreover, what the theory suggests is virtually physically impossible. The Jewish historian Josephus tells how he had three acquaintances who had been crucified and removed from their crosses, but despite the best medical attention two of the three died anyway (*Life* 75. 420-1). The extent of Jesus' tortures was such that he could never have survived the crucifixion and entombment. The suggestion that a man so critically wounded then went on to appear to the disciples on various occasions in Jerusalem and Galilee is pure fantasy.

4. **Less contrived.** The Apparent Death Hypothesis, especially in its conspiratorial versions, can become enormously contrived. We're invited to imagine secret societies, stealthily administered potions, conspiratorial alliances between Jesus' disciples and members of the Sanhedrin, and so forth, all with not of scrap of evidence in support.

5. **Disconfirmed by fewer accepted beliefs.** The Apparent Death Hypothesis is massively disconfirmed by medical facts concerning what would happen to a person who had been scourged and crucified, and by the unanimous evidence Jesus did not continue among his disciples after his death.

6. **Exceeds other hypotheses in fulfilling conditions (1) – (5).** This theory also is hardly a standout! For that reason it has virtually no defenders among New Testament historians today.

Displaced Body Hypothesis

In one of the few modern Jewish attempts to deal with the facts concerning Jesus' resurrection, Joseph Klausner in 1922 proposed that Joseph of Arimathea placed Jesus' body in his tomb temporarily, due to the lateness of the hour and the closeness of his family tomb to the place of Jesus' execution, but then he moved the corpse later to the criminals' common graveyard. Unaware of the displacement of the body, the disciples upon finding the tomb empty inferred that Jesus was risen from the dead. Although no scholars defend Klausner's hypothesis today, some popular authors have attempted to revive it.

1. **Explanatory scope.** The Displaced Body Hypothesis has narrow explanatory scope. It tries to explain the empty tomb but says nothing about the

post-mortem appearances and the origin of the disciples' belief in Jesus' resurrection. Independent hypotheses must be adopted to explain the full scope of the evidence.

2. EXPLANATORY POWER. Klausner's hypothesis has no explanatory power with regard to either the appearances or the origin of the Christian faith. As for the empty tomb, the hypothesis faces an obvious problem: since Joseph and any servants with him knew what they had done with the corpse, the theory is at a loss to explain why the disciples' error wasn't corrected once they began to proclaim Jesus' resurrection—unless, that is, one resorts to contrived conjectures to save the day, such as Joseph and his servants' sudden deaths!

It might be said that Jesus' corpse would have no longer been identifiable. That is, in fact, not true. Jewish burial practices typically involved digging up the bones of the deceased a year later and placing them in an ossuary. So gravesites, even for criminals, were carefully noted. But the objection misses the point. The earliest Jewish/Christian disputes about Jesus' resurrection were not over the location of Jesus' grave or the identity of the corpse but over why the tomb was empty. Had Joseph displaced the body, the Jewish/Christian controversy would have been different.

3. PLAUSIBILITY. The hypothesis is implausible for a number of reasons. So far as we can rely on Jewish sources, the criminals' graveyard was only 50 to 600 yards from the site of Jesus' crucifixion. Jewish practice, furthermore, was to bury executed criminals on the day of their execution, so that's what Joseph would have wanted to accomplish. Therefore, Joseph could and would have placed the body directly in the criminals' graveyard, thereby eliminating any need to move it later or defile his own family tomb. Indeed, Jewish law did not even *permit* the body to be moved later, except to the family tomb. Joseph had adequate time for a simple burial.

4. LESS CONTRIVED. The theory is mildly contrived in ascribing to Joseph motives and activities for which we have no evidence at all. It becomes really contrived if we have to start inventing things like Joseph's sudden death in order to save the hypothesis.

5. DISCONFIRMED BY FEWER ACCEPTED BELIEFS. The theory suffers disconfirmation from what we know about Jewish burial procedures for criminals mentioned above.

6. EXCEEDS OTHER HYPOTHESES IN FULFILLING CONDITIONS (1) – (5). Again, no historian seems to share this estimation.

Hallucination Hypothesis

In his book *The Life of Jesus, Critically Examined* (1835), David Strauss proposed that the resurrection appearances were merely hallucinations on the part of the disciples. The most prominent defender of this view today is the German New Testament critic Gerd Lüdemann. How does the Hallucination Hypothesis fare when assessed by our criteria?

1. EXPLANATORY SCOPE. The Hallucination Hypothesis has narrow explanatory scope. It says nothing to explain the empty tomb. Therefore, one must either deny the fact of the empty tomb (and the burial as well) or conjoin some *independent* hypothesis to the Hallucination Hypothesis to account for the empty tomb.

The Hallucination Hypothesis also says nothing to explain the origin of the disciples' belief in Jesus' resurrection. Simply postulating post-mortem visions of Jesus on the part of the disciples does not explain why they believed he was risen from the dead. To increase the plausibility of the Hallucination Hypothesis some scholars have made a great deal out of the alleged similarities between the post-mortem appearances of Jesus and visions of recently departed loved ones by the bereaved. But the overriding lesson of such intriguing stories is that the bereaved do not, as a result of such experiences, however real and tangible they may seem, conclude the deceased has returned physically to life—rather the deceased is seen in the afterlife. As Wright observes, for someone in the ancient world visions of the deceased are not evidence the person is alive, but evidence he is dead!

Moreover, in a Jewish context other more appropriate interpretations of such experiences than resurrection are close at hand. Given the current Jewish beliefs about life after death, the disciples, if they were to project hallucinations of Jesus, would have seen Jesus in heaven or in glory, where the souls of the righteous dead were believed to abide until the final resurrection. And such visions would not have led to belief in Jesus' resurrection. At most, it would have only led the disciples to say Jesus had been assumed into heaven, not raised from the dead.

In the Old Testament figures such as Enoch and Elijah were portrayed as not having died but as having been taken directly into heaven. In an extra-biblical Jewish writing called *The Testament of Job* (40) the story is told of two children killed in the collapse of a house. When the rescuers clear away the rubble the bodies of the children are nowhere to be found. Meanwhile, their mother sees a vision of the two children glorified in heaven where they have been taken up by God. It needs to be emphasized that for a Jew an assumption into heaven is not the same as a resurrection. Assumption is the taking of someone bodily out of this world into heaven. Resurrection is the raising up of a dead man in the space-time universe. They are distinct ideas.

Thus, even given hallucinations, belief in Jesus' resurrection remains unexplained in the Hallucination Hypothesis. Therefore, it has unacceptably narrow explanatory scope.

2. EXPLANATORY POWER. The Hallucination Hypothesis does nothing to explain the empty tomb and the origin of the disciples' belief in Jesus' resurrection. But, what about the appearances?

Suppose Peter was one of those individuals who experienced a vision of a deceased loved one or experienced a guilt-induced vision, as Lüdemann imagines. Would this suffice to explain the resurrection appearances? Not really, for the diversity of the appearances bursts the bounds of anything found in the psychological casebooks. Jesus appeared not just one time, but many times; not at just one locale and circumstance but at a variety of places and under a variety of circumstances; not to just one individual, but to different persons; not just to individuals, but to various groups; not just to believers but to unbelievers and even enemies. Positing a chain reaction among the disciples won't solve the problem because people like James and Paul don't stand in the chain. Those who would explain the resurrection appearances psychologically are compelled to construct a composite picture by cobbling together different unrelated cases of hallucinatory experiences, which only serves to underline the fact there's nothing like the resurrection appearances in the psychological casebooks.

3. PLAUSIBILITY. Lüdemann attempts to make his Hallucination Hypothesis plausible by psychoanalysis of Peter and Paul. He believes they both had guilt complexes which found release in hallucinations of Jesus. But Lüdemann's psychoanalysis is implausible for three reasons: *First*, Lüdemann's use of depth psychology is based upon theories of Jung and Freud which are highly disputed. *Second*, there is insufficient data to psychoanalyze Peter and Paul. Psychoanalysis is difficult enough to carry out even with patients on the couch, so to speak, but it's next to impossible with historical figures. For that reason the attempt to write psycho-biography is rejected by historians today. Finally, the evidence we do have suggests Paul did *not* struggle with a guilt complex as Lüdemann supposes.

Nearly 50 years ago the Swedish scholar Krister Stendahl pointed out that Western readers have tended to interpret Paul in light of Martin Luther's struggles with guilt and sin. But Paul experienced no such struggle. Stendahl writes:

> *Contrast Paul, a very happy and successful Jew, one who can say "'s to righteousness under the Law (I was) blameless'"(Phil. 3.6). That is what he says. He experiences no troubles, no problems, no qualms of conscience. He is a star pupil, the student to get the thousand dollar graduate scholarship in Gamaliel's Seminary... Nowhere in Paul's writings is there any indication... that psychologically Paul had some problem of conscience.*[10]

---

10 Krister Stendahl, "Paul among Jews and Gentiles," in *Paul among Jews and Gentiles* (Philadelphia: Fortesss Press, 1976), pp. 12-13.

To justify his portrait of a guilt-ridden Paul, Lüdemann is forced to interpret Romans 7 in terms of Paul's pre-Christian experience. But this interpretation is rejected by almost all commentators since the late 1920s. So, Lüdemann's ideas are positively implausible.

A second respect in which the Hallucination Hypothesis is implausible is its taking the appearances to be merely visionary experiences. Lüdemann recognizes the Hallucination Hypothesis depends on the presupposition that what Paul experienced on the Damascus Road was the same as what all the *other* disciples experienced, but this presupposition is groundless. By including himself in the list of eyewitnesses to Christ's resurrection appearances, Paul is in no way implying they were all just like the appearance to him. Many of Paul's opponents in Corinth denied he was a true apostle, so Paul is anxious to include himself with the other apostles who had seen Christ. Paul is trying to bring his experience up to the objectivity and reality of theirs, not to pull their experience down to merely visionary experiences.

4. Less contrived. Lüdemann's version of the Hallucination Hypothesis is contrived in a number of ways. It assumes the disciples fled back to Galilee after Jesus' arrest, Peter was so obsessed with guilt he projected a hallucination of Jesus, the other disciples were also prone to hallucinations, and Paul had a struggle with the Jewish law and a secret attraction to Christianity.

5. Disconfirmed by fewer accepted beliefs. Some of the accepted beliefs of New Testament scholars today tend to disconfirm the Hallucination Hypothesis, at least as Lüdemann presents it. For example, scholars believe Jesus received an honorable burial by Joseph of Arimathea; Jesus' tomb was discovered empty by women; psycho-analysis of historical figures is not feasible; Paul was basically content with his life under the Jewish law; and the New Testament makes a distinction between a mere vision and a resurrection appearance.

6. Exceeds other hypotheses in fulfilling conditions (1) – (5). The Hallucination Hypothesis remains a live option today and in that respect has outstripped its rivals. But the question is whether it outstrips the Resurrection Hypothesis.

The Resurrection Hypothesis

We've seen how poorly the typical explanations of the empty tomb, the post-mortem appearances, and the origin of the disciples' faith fare when assessed by standard criteria for testing historical hypotheses. They're especially weak when it comes to explanatory scope and power and are often highly implausible.

But does the Resurrection Hypothesis do any better at explaining the evidence?

1. EXPLANATORY SCOPE. The Resurrection Hypothesis has greater explanatory scope than explanations like the Hallucination Hypothesis or the Displaced Body Hypothesis precisely by explaining all three of the main facts at issue, whereas these rival hypotheses explain at most one.

2. EXPLANATORY POWER. This is perhaps the greatest strength of the Resurrection Hypothesis. If Jesus rose from the dead, the tomb would have been empty. The disciples should have seen appearances of Jesus alive. And they would have come to believe in his resurrection.

3. PLAUSIBILITY. The plausibility of Jesus' resurrection grows exponentially once we consider it in its historical context, namely, Jesus' unparalleled life and radical personal claims, and in its philosophical context, namely, the evidence for God's existence. Once one embraces the view God exists, the hypothesis God raised Jesus from the dead is no more implausible than its rivals.

4. LESS CONTRIVED. The Resurrection Hypothesis possesses great explanatory scope and power, but some scholars have charged that it is contrived. Being contrived is a matter of how many new suppositions a hypothesis must make which are not implied by existing knowledge.

So defined however, it's hard to see why the Resurrection Hypothesis is extraordinarily contrived. It requires only one new supposition: that God exists. Surely its rival hypotheses require many new suppositions. For example, the Conspiracy Hypothesis requires us to suppose the moral character of the disciples was defective, which is certainly not implied by already existing knowledge; the Apparent Death Hypothesis requires the supposition that the centurion's lance thrust into Jesus' side was just a superficial poke or is an unhistorical detail in the narrative, which again goes beyond existing knowledge; the Hallucination Hypothesis requires us to suppose some sort of emotional preparation of the disciples which predisposed them to project visions of Jesus alive, which is not implied by our knowledge. Such examples could be multiplied.

It should be noted too that scientific hypotheses regularly include the supposition of the existence of new entities, such as quarks, strings, gravitons, black holes, and the like, without those theories being characterized as contrived. Moreover, for the person who already believes in God, the Resurrection Hypothesis doesn't even introduce the new supposition of God's existence. So, the Resurrection Hypothesis cannot be said to be contrived simply in virtue of the number of new suppositions it introduces.

If our hypothesis is contrived then it must be for other reasons. Philosophers of science have found it notoriously difficult to explain what it is exactly that makes a hypothesis contrived. A hypothesis deemed to be contrived seems to have an air of artificiality which can be sensed by those who are seasoned practitioners of the relevant science.

Now I think that the sense of discomfort which many people, *even Christians*, feel about appealing to God as part of an explanatory hypothesis for some phenomenon is that so doing has an air of artificiality. It just seems too easy when confronted with some unexplained phenomenon to throw up one's hands and say, "God did it!"

Is the hypothesis that "God raised Jesus from the dead" contrived in this sense? I don't think so. A supernatural explanation of the empty tomb, the resurrection appearances, and the origin of the Christian faith is not contrived given the context of Jesus' own unparalleled life, ministry, and personal claims. A supernatural hypothesis readily fits into such a context. It's also precisely because of this historical context that the Resurrection Hypothesis does not seem contrived when compared to miraculous explanations of other sorts: for example, that a "psychological miracle" occurred, causing normal men and women to become conspirators and liars who would be willingly martyred for their lies; or that a "biological miracle" occurred, which prevented Jesus' dying on the cross (despite the spear-thrust through his chest, and so forth). It is *these* miraculous hypotheses which strike us as artificial and contrived, not the Resurrection Hypothesis, which makes abundantly good sense in the context of Jesus' ministry and radical personal claims. Thus, it seems to me that the Resurrection Hypothesis cannot be characterized as excessively contrived.

5. DISCONFIRMED BY FEWER ACCEPTED BELIEFS. I can't think of any accepted beliefs which disconfirm the Resurrection Hypothesis—unless one thinks of, say, "Dead men do not rise" as disconfirmatory. But this generalization does nothing to disconfirm the hypothesis that God raised Jesus from the dead. We may consistently believe *both* that men do not rise naturally from the dead *and* that God raised Jesus from the dead. By contrast, rival theories are disconfirmed by accepted beliefs about, for example, the instability of conspiracies, the likelihood of death as a result of crucifixion, the psychological characteristics of hallucinatory experiences, and so forth, as we have seen.

6. EXCEEDS OTHER HYPOTHESES IN FULFILLING CONDITIONS (1) – (5). There's certainly little chance of any of the rival hypotheses' ever exceeding the Resurrection Hypothesis in fulfilling the above conditions. The bewilderment of contemporary scholarship when confronted with the facts of the empty tomb, the resurrection appearances, and the origin of the Christian faith suggests that no better rival is anywhere on the horizon. Once you give up the prejudice against miracles it's hard to deny the resurrection of Jesus is the best explanation of the facts.

CONCLUSION

In conclusion therefore, three great, independently established facts—the empty tomb, the resurrection appearances, and the origin of the Christian faith—all point to the same marvelous conclusion: that God raised Jesus from the dead. Given that God exists, this conclusion cannot be barred to anyone seeking for the meaning to existence.

When, as a Fellow of the Alexander von Humboldt Foundation, I commenced my study of the historicity of Jesus' resurrection, I, as a Christian, already *believed* that the event had occurred. But it came as quite a surprise to me to discover how powerful a historical case can be mounted for its historicity. In particular, it was with stunned amazement that it gradually dawned upon me that the central facts undergirding the inference to Jesus' resurrection, namely, his empty tomb, his post-mortem appearances, and the origin of the disciples' belief in his resurrection—not to mention his crucifixion and burial in a tomb by Joseph—represent by far the majority viewpoint of historical scholars who have published on the subject. One's willingness to accept Jesus' resurrection as the best explanation of the facts is apt to hinge more upon one's openness to a supernatural worldview than upon purely historical considerations.